# On your feet

Written by Susan Frame

a Capstone company — publishers for children

All sorts of things can be worn on your feet.

## Off to the moon!

If you had been to the moon, you might have worn this sort of gear on your feet.

You need to keep fit if you are going to the moon. The men hopped up and down in this pair to keep fit in the rocket ship!

But they had big boots for hopping on the moon.

This is a boot mark on the moon.

# Geta

Geta are wooden.
They are worn in Japan.

Geta have 2 big 'teeth' on the bottom.
The teeth keep feet out of the mud.

They can be worn with socks.

This man sells geta in his shop.

# Footgear for fishers

Look at all the boots hanging up!

They are rubber and they are worn by fishers. See how long they are? They go right up to the hip, so they are good for fishing in deep rivers. The fisher's legs will not get soaking wet with this pair of boots on.

# Hard-cap boots

Feet will not get hurt if they are in a pair of hard-cap boots. Hard-cap boots have a solid tip. See the men with this sort of boot on? If a sharp thing hits a boot such as this, there will be no harm to the foot at all. Thank goodness for that!

# Summer gear

This summer footgear keeps feet high up and off the hot soil.

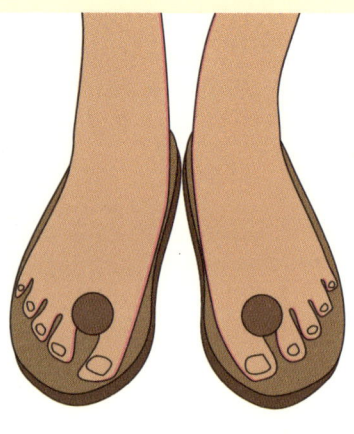

There are wooden pegs on top, but no cord at the back. Do you think it might be hard to keep them secure on your feet?

This sort of thing was worn a lot, years back, but it is not worn much now.

If you had a pair in silver, it said, "Look at how rich I am!"

This is a silver charm. You will have good luck if you pop it in your pocket.

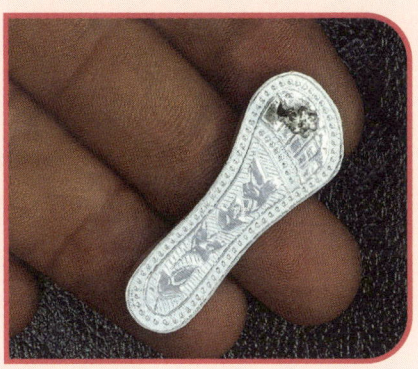

# Boots

Let's have a good look at boots. There are short boots and long boots. And boots for the rain.

There are boots with high heels and with not-so-high heels!
And a pair of cool silver boots.

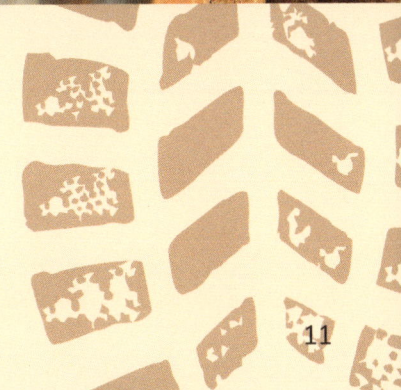

Your feet will not get too wet in this sort of boot. They keep out the chill, as well.

They are good for going up and down hills ...

... and for out on the farm ...

... and for running in wet mud.

This is a pair of boots worn by a queen in the 1800s. Look at all the buttons. They go on and on!

This is the queen in 1837. She was 18 years old.

The queen said she had better things to do than do up lots of buttons. So, in 1837, this pair of boots was formed for her. Not one button to do up!

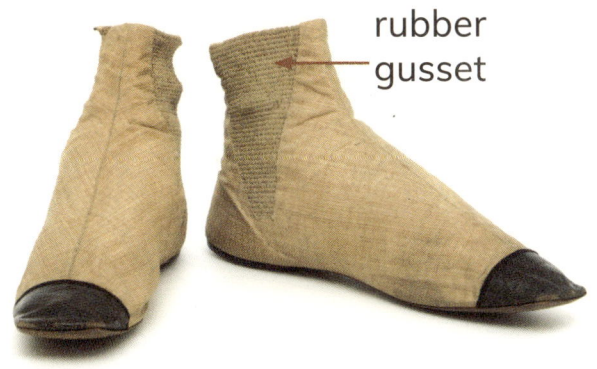

rubber gusset

The queen was seen out morning, noon and night in her boots. She popped them on and off. So quick!
There are lots of boots such as this in shops now – all thanks to the queen!

This is a pair of boots worn by a man in the 1600s. They sat high up his legs, at the mid-thigh mark. A man had long boots to keep his feet out of the mud and to keep the rain off.

# All sorts of heels

This is a pair of cork heels.

And, wow! That is a **high** pair of heels!

This heel is not too high.
It is a 'kitten' heel.

This is not a kitten heel, but it is good for a cat!

This pair of heels was worn by men in the 1700s.

Rich kings had lots of pairs of heels back then. Do you think they look good?

# Socks

Socks have been worn for years and years.

Far back, men had socks of fur and matted cow and goat hair.

Up until the 1700s, you had to be rich to have socks so no one but kings and queens had them. This king has long socks on.

This man was born in 1879. He was quick-witted and good at maths, but he did **not** have socks. Not one pair. Do you think that is odd?

Maths is my thing – not socks!

A thick pair of woollen socks will keep out the chill. They are good to have on with boots, too. They pad your feet so the boots do not rub.

Did you get up in the dark this morning? If so, check your feet! You might have odd socks on.

Oh no, look at this!

Well, get out your wool and darn it! It is good to fix your socks. You will have them for years if you do.

— darning

And if you cannot darn your socks ...

... cut off the bottoms.
Now you have a pair
of fingerless mittens.